Healthy Habits

Move and Run

Sue Barraclough

FRANKLIN WATTS
LONDON • SYDNEY

First published in 2010 by
Franklin Watts
338 Euston Road
London NW1 3BH

Franklin Watts Australia
Level 17/207 Kent Street
Sydney NSW 2000

Art director: Jonathan Hair
Series editor: Julia Bird
Design: Jane Hawkins

A CIP catalogue record for this
book is available from the
British Library.

ISBN 978 0 7496 9301 5

Dewey classification: 591.5'7

Picture credits: Ace Stock Ltd/Alamy: 10; Baxternator/istockphoto: front
cover t; Manfred Danegger/NHPA: 17; Tim Davis/Corbis: 21;
Mitch Diamond/Alamy: 16; DLILLC/Corbis: front cover b, 14;
Peter Frank/Corbis: 13; Nick Garbutt/NHPA: 7.
T Kitchen & V Hurst/NHPA: 11; Imagemore Co Ltd/Corbis: 2, 8;
Image Source/Corbis: 18; Phillipe Lissac/Godong/Corbis: 23.
Neil McAlister/Alamy: 4; Ross Nolly/NHPA: 9; Jari Peltomaki/NHPA:
5; Andy Rowse/NHPA: 19; Ant Strack/Corbis: 6;
Thinkstock/Corbis: 20; Terry Vine/Blend Images/Corbis: 22.
David Wall/Alamy: 15; Dave Watts/NHPA: 1, 12.

Every attempt has been made to clear copyright. Should there be any inadvertent omission,
please apply to the publisher for rectification.

Printed in China

Franklin Watts is a division of
Hachette Children's Books,
an Hachette UK company.
www.hachette.co.uk

Contents

Moving around

Humans and other animals need to move around every day to stay **healthy**.

Moving and running keeps your body strong and **fit.**

This owl moves its powerful wings to swoop down to catch its **prey.**

Wild animals need to be able to move around to find or hunt for food. They also need to find water and **shelter**.

Bodies and energy

Your body is working all the time. Your body uses food to give it **energy** to do work. You breathe all the time and your **heart** pumps blood around your body to keep it active.

You breathe in and out, even when you are sleeping.

Think about it

Can you feel your heart working?

This lizard is sunbathing on a rock. A lizard needs to warm its body in the Sun to give it energy so that it can move.

A lizard's long tail helps it to balance as it moves.

Muscles and bones

Your body is made of moving parts. Your bones **support** your body and give it its shape. This shape is called your **skeleton**. Your **muscles** are stretchy parts that work with your bones to move your body.

This ballet dancer is using her bones and muscles to stretch her arms and point her toes.

8

Most animals use bones and muscles to make them move, too. Insects and spiders do not have bones like us. Instead, they have an outer casing that protects their body.

A spider's legs can bend to help it cling or climb.

Q How many legs does a spider have?

A Eight.

Moving parts

You can walk or run to move from place to place. Walking and running help to **exercise** your body and make it stronger.

Running makes our heart and **lungs** work hard.

Think about it

How do you feel when you have been running?

Different animals use different body parts such as legs, wings or **fins** to get from place to place.

A butterfly flaps its wings to fly from flower to flower.

11

Strong legs

A kangaroo has very strong back legs and small arms. A kangaroo uses its strong back legs to hop very fast.

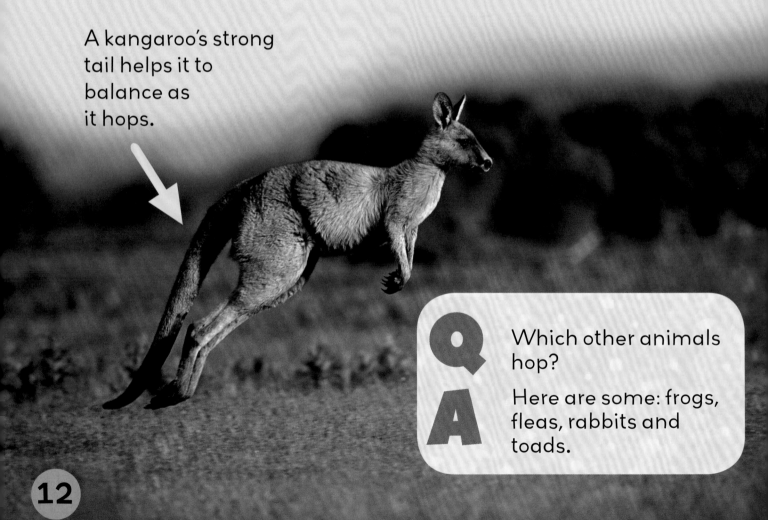

A kangaroo's strong tail helps it to balance as it hops.

Q Which other animals hop?

A Here are some: frogs, fleas, rabbits and toads.

Your legs support your body. Legs need to be strong and healthy to help you run, jump and climb.

This girl is using the strong muscles in her legs to push herself up the ladder.

13

Strong arms

This orang-utan has long, strong arms. It uses its arms to climb and swing in trees to find food.

Orang-utans eat fruit and leaves from the trees.

As you use and move parts of your body, you make them stronger.

This girl needs strong hands and arms to swing on the bars.

Think about it

What is your favourite kind of exercise?

15

Moving and growing

A baby needs to learn how to stand and how to walk. A baby needs to use his or her legs to make them stronger.

This baby needs help to stand up.

This young stork is moving and stretching its wings. It moves and stretches its wings to make them stronger so that it can learn to fly.

Storks learn to fly when they are about two months old.

Q Which bird can fly the fastest?

A A peregrine falcon.

17

Moving and learning

This girl is learning how to write.

You learn how to move your body by watching other people. You learn by trying to do things. You learn by **practising** movements.

18

Young wild animals need to learn how to hunt for food. Lions learn by watching their mothers hunt and copying what they do.

Think about it

Why do young animals play-fight?

These young lions are practising their hunting skills.

19

Moving in water

When you swim, you use your arms and legs to push you through the water. Swimming is good exercise for your whole body.

Swimming is good for building strong muscles.

A dolphin lives in water. Its body is shaped to move through the water. Its tail and fins push its body along.

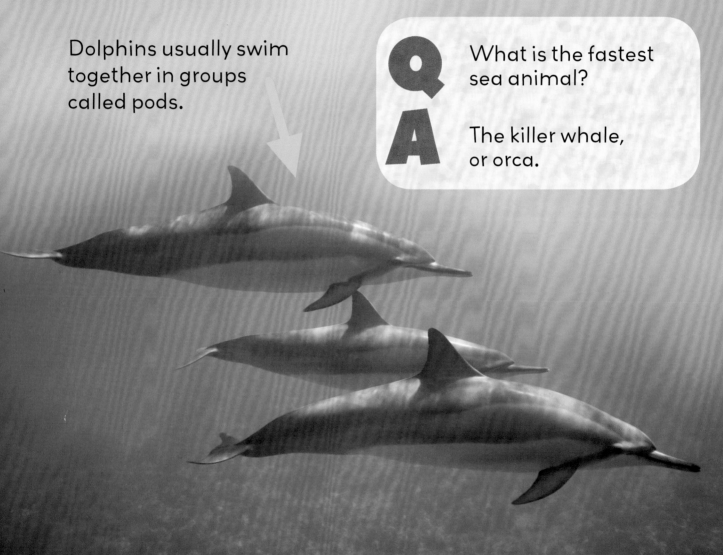

Dolphins usually swim together in groups called pods.

Q What is the fastest sea animal?

A The killer whale, or orca.

Keep moving!

- ✓ Aim to do one hour of exercise or active play every day. Try to do a mixture of different exercises such as running, swimming and climbing.

- ✓ When you can, walk or cycle instead of travelling by car.

- ✓ Eat a healthy mixture of different foods, especially fruit and vegetables.

- ✓ Drink plenty of water.

Riding a bike is a good way to keep fit.

✓ Notice how your body feels as you exercise. This will help you learn how much you can do.

✗ Try not to spend more than two hours a day watching TV or playing computer games.

✓ Have fun! Choose activities that you enjoy doing.

You need to keep more than your fingers active to stay fit!

Glossary

energy something that makes things move, change or grow.
exercise using your muscles to keep fit.
fins the parts of a fish that help push it through the water.
fit if you are fit your body works well and feels strong.
healthy strong and active.
heart a part of the body in the chest that pumps blood.
lungs body parts in the chest that are used for breathing.
muscles stretchy parts of the body that work with the bones.
practising doing something again and again.
prey an animal that is eaten by another animal.
shelter something that gives protection from the weather or from danger.
skeleton the bones that hold up and protect our body.
support to hold something up and stop it falling.

Index

24